# Back Through Interruption

*Poems by*

Kate Northrop

The Kent State University Press

*Kent & London*

*To my mother and father—and for Bill*

© 2002 by Kate Northrop

Library of Congress Catalog Card Number 2002002219
ISBN 0-87338-741-4
Manufactured in the United States of America

06  05  04  03  02    5  4  3  2  1

The Wick Poetry First Book Series is sponsored by the Stan and Tom Wick Poetry Program and the Department of English at Kent State University.

Library of Congress Cataloging-in-Publication Data
Northrop, Kate 1969–
       Back through interruption: poems / by Kate Northrop.
              p.       cm.—(Wick poetry first book series)
       ISBN 0-87338-741-4 (pbk.: alk paper)
       I. Title.   II. Series.
PS3614.079 B33    2002
811'.6—dc21                                                        2002002219

British Library Cataloging-in-Publication data are available.

# Contents

Three

## Acknowledgments

A number of poems in this book were published previously (often in earlier versions). Grateful acknowledgment is made to the editors of the following journals for permission to reprint these poems: "The Murderer" and "The Geranium" *American Poetry Review;* "Story," "The Servant Girl," "Two Stories with Wish & Leap" *Black Warrior Review;* "Skating," *Controlled Burn;* "Milk," *Dark Horse;* "Aaron Davis," "Hiding," *Louisiana Literature;* "Landscape with Abandoned Trash," *The Massachusetts Review;* "Susans," *Michigan Quarterly Review;* "The Visitor," *Mudfish;* "Gardening," "The Affair," *Northwest Review;* "Brides," *Painted Bride Quarterly;* "The End of Winter," "Iowa & Other Accidents," *Poet Lore;* "There's a Man," "On the Hotel Balcony," *Raritan;* "The Dead," *Rattle;* and "Late Aubade & Explanation," "Ahkmatova and Modigliani," *Third Coast.*

The anecdote about the open window in "Akhmatova & Modigliani" was taken from Roberta Reeder's biography, *Anna Akhmatova: Poet and Prophet,* 1944. The third section of "Affair with Various Endings" refers to the elegy "Andree Rexroth" by Kenneth Rexroth. "Paula's Mother's Garden" is dedicated to Paula Deitz, as the poem began with a story she told me and which—for the purposes of this book—has been much changed. The original story can be found in Deitz's essay, "My Mother's Garden" in *The Writer in the Garden,* edited by Jane Garmey. "There's a Man" is dedicated to Emily Powell. "The Dead" is dedicated to the memory of my grandmother, Dorthea C. Zettler.

Some poems in this book were first published together in *Evening,* a limited edition by Aralia Press. I thank Michael Peich for his beautiful work and his encouragement.

Thanks also to Maggie Anderson, Stephen Berg, Christine Brooks, Jough Dempsey, Lynn Emanuel, Andrew Hudgins, and Steven Polgar for the time and attention they gave this manuscript.

For years of friendship, I am grateful to Allison Ramler, N. F. Ingram, Jennifer Kelland, Paula Hatfield, Luanne Smith, and my sister Molly Ayers Northrop. And thank-yous to my mother and father.

# One

## Iowa & Other Accidents

There was snow that afternoon covering the road
which twisted toward the secret
of water, the mysterious surge

of sludge & loam, the living
Mississippi, unlike the rest of the Midwest,

drawing itself through landscape. There was an appointment
   you were keeping

in Moline: a cheap hotel, booze, a little blow. On the Lower
   East Side, a woman

spills her martini, makes a gesture
like erasure, or regret. It was almost Christmas.
In the rear view

suddenly, the car you will always describe as *oncoming*
must have slipped into a skid

and now, rising up over the bank,
it startles you—that reflection. In Moline

the maid corners the bed, straightens the clean
line of sheet. Almost Christmas. On the road,
swirls of snow. On the road

the car hovering behind you, a witness,
unfortunate & so unlike the audience permitted
the distance of fictions, the artifice

of plot. And worse, of course, the law

of cause & effect: *I looked up,
it started to fall.* You must attach

subject to verb, must say
*I saw,* and did, in your rear view, the car you'd thought
    nothing of,

the gray sedan lifting slowly from the common snow,
turning, and the accident
always there, about to happen.

## Story with Forest, Girl & Boy

In the black forest a girl, of course, and a boy are kneeling at
    a crossroads.
They are making matchbooks speak.

In the village at a table hewn from oak, a man, sitting alone,
    sips a glass of Slivovitz. What's he doing

with his head in his hands? Is it the witch of description
visiting him, describing the failures
one by one, pulling them out until his head pounds? He hears

something, a whispering

which is the sound of flames far away catching
though he mistakes it
for rodents, several blind mice

scurrying behind the closed pantry door. It sounds
like a secret, like something

locked in the heart. Meanwhile, at the edge of the woods,
the boy and the girl are holding hands. A gnarled
and knotty pine goes up, it goes up

in a sleeve of smoke that sweeps its way out across the sky.
Down here, it catches. It's going to catch

the boy and the girl, their faces
growing hot, trees gleaming in their eyes.

## The Affair

Was there ever an option? For example,
    how could she have known? How could she

have *not* been on the train
pulling into the station, a constant
arrival, repeating itself

in the blue Russian wind? The good people
keep waiting. They're beginning
departures, shifting position,

getting ready. One woman
slips on the ice,

and the wind lifts the lightest strands of her hair

but this is not the disaster. The man, the one
    who concerns us, he's there
among them, lighting

a cigarette, and right now

a stranger to me, the reader, and to her, the woman
in her assigned seat, married,

traveling without family. Earlier
    in her room, in the open unblemished morning,

when she was folding her clothes
into quarters, brushing out a blouse,
wasn't she at that moment

a good wife? Or was she always
moving toward this, accruing traits, characteristics

that would make her *the kind of woman who*—

The rest is dirt. You already know it. He steps
into the warm compartment, she lifts
her face, recognizes that

which will undo her. Soon they leave
their homes. They touch, fuck; they wreck each other

with jealousy, with eventual
loneliness. I don't love him there at the splintered
end of the novel,

but in the station? In the station, it's possible,
I do. When he's alone

and turning to watch the train
scheduled in the distance, coming on, pulling through.

## Two Stories with Wish & Leap

Nothing much is known about the girl—
if she hesitated, how she looked
up there on the railing, like a coward
or a victim? We liken her at times

to a leaf: quivering, pale. It's the dress
torn, the hands already in memory, already
permanent, that have her on the bridge
leaning toward water. We weren't awake

at the story's end but know in daylight
to trust the bridge or trust the river.
Either way a leaving of the mind
behind: the boy, the scene,

the car. I've looked like her at the river.
Our barn folded, washed out into the flood,
its roof a tilted hat the water wore.
What belongs inside, turned out: my couch

rising off the porch rolled four legs up
and Joe mistook it for a cow. He shot it
twice. What kind of man mistakes *couch*
for *cow?* A broken stick with which

I draw my name, the date, *I was here.*
I wished him upon the water. Along with bed
and bureau, a gun, a dirty hat.
The sky is littered with the river.

When I touch the plaque, cool memorial,
leaves crane slightly and silt shifts.
It was the wrong car, the wrong time, the hands
that kept occurring on the wheel, in the hair

of the girl that kept occurring while the bridge
in the name of the father of the town
was steel unyielding over moonlight.
A sudden lightness of the legs?

A drawing back midfall? Or a sound
like leaves unfolding in the ear?
Either way we trust the fact—which is
absence—a girl inside the water.

## Akhmatova & Modigliani

It's Paris, 1911, during her first marriage
and usually they meet

in the gardens where they speak
of angles and art, recite
passages of Verlaine. Behind them

children cartwheel through trees. In the days to come
he will paint her face, austere
as architecture, preserve it

in fifteen portraits though the portraits
go missing. Today they've arranged

to visit his studio. The morning rain
has given way to sun
brightening the courtyard. There's Akhmatova

with a dozen roses, red
as a cut. She calls up to him;
he isn't home. She shifts

foot to foot. And what happens? You know
what happens. It's 1910 and soon they will murder
lovers like these, murder husbands

and sons. They take the roads away. But first

in the courtyard
she throws each long rose, one
by one, through the open window.

She stands there in that moment, listening.

The years ahead pick up their dark bags.
They move closer. There's a slight rise in the silence

then nothing. Someone shuts a cupboard
in a kitchen, and a stray cat

slips quickly through the flowerpots.

## The End of Winter

March, thin pane between in
and outside, is a window against which

I lean up and I can tell you, I am tired
of my body, the way it knocks
against the walls, the way it makes

the floorboards creak. I want to go out

over it, the landscape unbroken
and travel the way we travel into memory:
unnoticed and noticing, unseen. Look,

the daffodils again are a stroke
of yellow through the park. Paper whites,
pale narcissus. Spring's a long

exhalation, an arching
slope into summer,

and the girls will be beautiful, the girls—

I want to go out but cannot let go
of those thin blue
afternoons, the secret

devastating cigarettes, and the little
funeral procession I saw

disappearing down the avenue into the rain.

## On the Hotel Balcony

— sundown, Miami

They've come through the sliding door,
her first,

to share what they're carrying: wine
and local fruit. He brings a pencil out, a pad of paper
and sketches the oranges,

the open knife. He sketches her feet up over the sea

and watches while she turns
softer, touched by light which turns the leaves
watery orange—

It turns her face

so he sticks to particulars: the long sweep, underside
    of thigh, the hollow

below the ankle, a sharp curve
of bone. Still, she's looking away at a beach house,

a yellow bicycle. It's the moment afterward
that's taken and set them adrift. Each

will go over the ocean

and it's no matter if the sketch
bears a certain resemblance,

it cannot attach her to the world
nor can he now
say her name quietly enough

to draw her back through interruption,
make her stay.

# The Suicides

## Part One—Morning

Girls in the morning paper. Dead girls
and still they insist on smiling:
the V-neck gowns, the earrings, the pearls.
It's early. It's unbelievable. They were *just girls.*

The senior poses, the photos from a month before
prove these five were happy, a semblance
of happiness. The photos seemed honest in a wallet,
in gilded frame, peaceful on piano top.

It's now we second-guess those smiles
(the newsprint gone granular and gray) and second-guess
the perfect surface of a face. What's wrong
with the picture is what's wrong with a fire, soundless

in a fireplace: the hollowness of pipes,
the gas flame and logs that strangely stay unburned.
The girls aren't telling, aren't talking.
Left to my own device, what's inside a girl?

Part Two—Night

An end to the pitch and moan of housewives,
the conversations hushed & urgent in the coffee shop.
Ethel, Our Lady of the Grill, restocks the sugar,
marries the ketchup and things go on:

the bank goes on displaying time, temperature falling,
the traffic light goes on blinking, clicking
slower now, red to green for the last car
at 3 a.m. The questions we asked all day

remain unanswered, contain themselves, do not burn up.
Bodies are coverings. They cover secrets. They covered up
the girls and cover now the man who sleeps beside me.
The body like a boat. The body sealed.

It doesn't matter how I feel. Beneath the leaves
of pachysandra, the insects are falling out of order
and the girls come back: this way, a chorus wailing;
that way, summer dresses, ankle straps & heels.

## The Visitor

Down the hill, in the field of sweet alfalfa, they're
    freezing each other, the children

playing tag and I'm up at the house, I'm
in the picture window, thin
and distant like the glimpse

of a surfacing fish. What dark water
the house is, behind me, settling
into evening. Dusk

and there are, of course, fireflies. Tell me,
what was your name? When you visited once,

by the back road where stones glowed pale
in the moonlight, I was too young, I still thought
I belonged to the world. But now

quartered in this house, watching the neighbors' children
turn to dusk, I feel
I'm ready. Come back

and bring your finest wine, the oldest bottle.
Bring that strange dusty book you were reading.

## Her Apology & Lament

I was busy in the kitchen. I didn't hear
the door open. I didn't hear him standing there.

Snow was sliding over magnolia leaves.

I didn't plan what happened. I was still your wife.
I hadn't planned anything.

   Once—after his third return—he said
*Why don't you let more light in here?*
I heard correctly. I heard *choose,*

so I knew I was his sweetheart. That,
   and my body started to hurt

in certain places, the inner walls
of the rib cage, for example. The skin
tightened across my palms.

           ·

The worst? I knew what the future held:
I would be judged
and what was individual

would collapse under the burden
of a story. But aren't there other kinds

of decisions? A man may leave his family, flee
for Tahiti, the colors of the southern Pacific. Or a heretic
chooses a new religion. God

enters the body, and the soul feels itself
unburdened, rising—

           ·

It was February, the start of March. Increasingly
I needed him. Even before it was over, I was worried; I was waiting
for the next time.

I tell myself

*Love's only the need to believe*
*in a power greater than the self, the need to surrender*

*to attraction to the convenience of mystery.*

But even now, I can enter
the memory. Everything is

as it was: snow drifting across the field, the car door

closing, and then his step
on the porch, in the hall, over floorboards.

*Affair with Various Endings*

I. Kempton, Pennsylvania

Perhaps the last of the light
lifting this evening from the field of wheat

means something. Perhaps the view
includes us, and we are not errors
in the landscape

or meant to be erased. The painter, it's true,
prefers not to preserve
our figures in the brush

of hills layered into green. Perhaps he too
is careless with the truth. What lies

have you had to tell to land you here

outside Kempton, with the creek rising behind us?
How did the story sound? If I say *your hand
on my thigh,* the truck still idles

beneath us, tracks in the frozen road

that months from now will thaw
& heave. If I say *your mouth*
and the deer begin drifting

across the field, who's to say
we didn't call them out—their figures shadowy,

their eyes gem-like and glittering?

## II. Undine

It was too urgent being human.
You ordered drinks, gestured
with your hands, told stories

and the more I knew

the more I was frightened. Those evenings
the air came unpinned, got lost
in autumn & dusk, in the leaves

at the edge of the field. And weren't the edges themselves
vanishing? When you walked to the barn,
where the cats had gone in,

taken to rafters. I heard your footsteps
moving the gravel, the ice
in your glass of vodka.

      I listened like that
for the ends of things: the last of the cars, the headlights crossing
our bedroom. I listened
to your breathing

      but rooms kept turning in places
I could not ignore. I left because I loved you
without reserve. Because I would not be allowed

to keep you with me in the world.

III. "Kings River Canyon"

Because when you read it your voice shakes,
    breaks over the last words,

Because in the Pennsylvania Hospital
at 8th and Spruce, surgeons have split open your chest
and with instruments

are cutting your heart,

And because I wanted to hurt them, my students, because they never
    get older, but return each year

refreshed, blond—

I read the poem: Rexroth walking back through the canyon
where twenty years before he had slept
with his new wife

at the beginning of autumn.
It was her birthday

and they lay there on the hard earth,

the stream running beside
and the walls soaring up

to hold them there. Maybe
he made love to her, the air
chilling their skin

or maybe that was the disease

beginning even then, gathering itself deep
inside her body, considering
the distance between itself

and the surface.
    There was no path.
They'd cut their way into the canyon

where eighteen years later,
    a highway's been blasted through. *Eighteen years*
he writes *ground to pieces.*

*I am more alone than I ever imagined.*

*You are dead.* And in the mechanical
cool of the classroom
I felt it grip me:

how it will be without you
when I'm fifty-five, sixty,

in the beginning of winter, in the first
waves of snow. I'll watch the slow drag
of the Schuylkill

or I'll go to the garden where we met,
the leaves spinning down
into the empty fountain,

where I will never see you,
not again, not your hands, your face,
or hear aloud the way

you said my name. I'll turn
and turn again,

but you'll be gone, nothing filling up your place.

# Two

## The Advice of the Dream

The dream that escaped the dream
went to live in a field. It was happy,
being undreamt, snapping dead sticks to add
to the fire it warmed itself around.

All night, in order to stay awake, it counted places.
How many oceans? How many mountain trails
lined with fern and woodchip, with flower?
And how many windows in the evening strangely lit?

The arms. Avenues. Estuaries
of ancient rivers, markets of spice, cumin
shifting in the barrels like sand,
like the desert, like anything in the open air.

It happens that the characters inside the dream
mill about, awkwardly, lost.
They've been knocked from the epic,
loosed from line of plot, from story.

The index cards have gone blank in their hands.
What's my line? When do I enter? And where should I stand?
Evenings in the field, there's the rustle
of autumnal husks, and beyond that,

a slight creek running. The advice of the dream?
It's important to stay unattached
to an actual happening. This makes you fleet-footed,
able to be everywhere in the world.

## Landscape with a Lake

Over & over you've returned, all summer,
   troubled—

circling the lake, unable to decide,

and seeing that now the poor
echoes of laughter, the last rising voice
has looked around, shuddered

& disappeared,
what will you do? The reeds, softened

by algae, draw back, and the torn pods of cattails,
which during the day
surrounded the lake, return

to dusk. It's a relief—isn't it?—not having
to be seen.

   (And do you feel less
obvious in the dark? Can you keep
forever, these secrets?)

       Say *I will return*
*to my wife* and there go the herons you saw earlier, there go

memories of herons. Say *I will not* and something inside slips,
the particular arrangements, the shapes
& layer of clouds. *Cirrus,*

*Cumulus*—these are the lovely names,
the children. All summer you've returned,

listened to the sounds of water, listened
for a voice, a decision. But now
the wind is gathering in the north,

and now it is somewhere behind you,
where the leaves already are falling,

and the snow is coming on—thick
& deep. We will not be here

very long. Do not
tell the truth. Don't leave me.

## Landscape with House at the Edge of a Field

What was it that you wanted to say?
  I've been waiting

and after all this time, nothing,
not a word. The geese

are crossing over
  and your picture's

on the table. Under the lamp. I won't remove it,
and the women who visit look sour, or snicker
like idiots.

  Where are you?
It shouldn't matter, I know. You were only

some trouble—a few drinks
in a rusted-out pickup—

but I believed. Now, over the rows
of long broken stalks,

the sky goes grey. And the husks, those uneasy
remnants, begin to scratch

and rustle. Soon I will open the door
of the house. I will go in.

## The Murderer

When he enters the room,
   the walls darken,

just slightly, and a cloud
covers the lake. But nobody notices. The party's
already started,

and our hosts, dreamlike, serve up the last
   of the summer cocktails

to gorgeous guests. Outside,
floating across the terrace, white petals. An old yacht
slides by. The murderer

is touching the cream pitcher. He circles
through conversations, then he is turning over
   his silver:

the salad fork, just once, the spoon. His hands
move exactly—cool, detached

like the light slanting lower across the lawn. Slowly,
   in October,

the body will surface, the body
will reveal itself

and though nobody knows yet, some women,
after the capture, will say *I could tell something
was different. I just kind of sensed it,*

but that's not true. Only the walls
knew he was sliding among us,
a secret celebrity, and trailing after him

drama, romance, disease.

## A Glimpse of You, a Vision

What else was I doing in the kitchen
 but watching?

For weeks I stood at the sink
long after the lights of the last car
had crossed the room. It was the end

of summer, and ahead, the hours
were shortening. I listened

in the dark where the curve of the faucet
glowed blue in the moonlight, familiar
& strange, like something

dredged up, like evidence. The wind stirred,

brushed the lowest branches of the oak
close against the house—and how else explain?—I knew it
the moment before,

then it was happening: You were there, sudden figure
at the window, your face a pale
white bloom, your shadow

vanishing in the yard through leaves.

## Her Body in the Landscape

First it was cursive—,
  a question mark, something humped with mud, sunk

deep in the Corbitt's marsh.
Then, over a day or two, it hardened

into bone, script. The trees, turning colors,
turned over it rising below. But

as yet, her body was a secret,

her murder blurred,
invisible. Evenings, when laughter came

ringing across the lake, it sounded thin

and distant, like a fork dropped
a moment before on a plate. The trees

leaned closer, perhaps to cover her,

but the body will not go through winter
undiscovered. Someone
stumbles upon it. Someone can't keep

a secret. Therefore,
the authorities will remove her

carefully from the marsh, from the years
  of indifferent weather,

from the stars that shine exactly
through the bare limbs of trees.

## Landscape with Abandoned Trash

The washer stopped where it tumbled to,
    down from the edge of the woods

into the gully and now several leaves sprout out
of the holes rust left. It's early autumn
and the rain,

falling through the trees, falls also

into the old machine; there's just enough light
to see by. Shadows

rustle in the corner
and further in, among hunks of mud, layers
of rotting leaves,

lay the remains of a mouse:
the skeleton

collapsed, the rib cage fanned out, partially
    broken out of form,
like a stutter. The bones,

more than the leaves, more than the walls
of the machine, the bones

hold the light, and through them
you hear echoes

from a brighter world—the sun

bleaching the sand, distant trumpets
& fanfare, the coronation

of a king.

## Inside the Room

There's not much to notice: against the far wall
    an old piano, and taped up beside it

a fly-specked old poster: *Our Wildlife
in Pennsylvania.* A few shadows

go over the floor, the dark
    abstractions attached

to the geese crying overhead, those keeping
to pattern. You move further in,
and what's outside slides away

as if down the sheer face of a cliff.
It's quiet. Your shoes pinch. Then through the doorway
returning in a long

full skirt, your mother, dead eight years, not quite

as you'd remembered: a little
giddy, heavier in the arms, but somewhat
    musical,

she who never sang coming forward smiling with a broom. *Are you
    almost done in here? Excuse me—*

so polite, then vanishing. It takes
a long time. The sky's overcast, a wind
rises against the walls,

and there's the sound of thunder approaching,
a heavy rain. Still, though the storm's

torrential, it's an occurrence

in weather, something you assume *happens,* meaning
   it begins

and ends. So you listen there at the edge
   of a great emptiness

for the arrival of silence,
the ending, the slow opening.

## Milk

There is something blue about it
and believe me, you can't trust it. Inside,

a wide field, sky, a few stones
by the road overgrown and out of that,
a city flowers, it breaks

into avenues and apartments. People meet each other
while strolling. *Good Day, Good Morning.* Later
they will couple,

they will clutch & cling, they will marry
& twist into strange
positions, strange in their beds,

in their own strange apartments. And later, years later,
there will be crickets, a kind of silence,

there will be pale stones in a field
of pale grass growing over.

## Paula's Mother's Garden

Why is it a violation?—Paula

picking the garden up, years
after the funeral, putting it elsewhere. Is it
your business

after all, where a garden
winds up?

You keep imagining
how it happened to Paula happening
to you: the perimeters of childhood

lifted up, cut away, like losing

a room—*because a garden*

*is a room*—and finding it assembled
elsewhere.
    Did you want to believe

you were unique? I remember your own mother
explaining the names: *hellebore, hydrangea,*
    *cleome*—

& Paula's mother too
in Paula's memory, *here is where she*— but where is *here*

after the separations,
the cardboard boxes of hostas packed
into the back of the station wagon, after

the re-attachments? Is it along the river, the garden
    as the garden

was conceived in Yardley?
Or is the garden elsewhere

reborn on a farm
in Jersey? The same plants in the same
arrangement: four quarters

circling the crepe myrtle, four borders
    of boxwood

filling out, casting shade over the violet
and viola. It would be good for you
to live more like that, indifferent,

without allegiances. The garden does not need
what you need: the comfort

of an individual, those lies,
those tired promises.

## The Geranium

How can you stand it—*looking* at things?
  For example, the geranium

out on the patio, the single pink
blossom in the sun? Or stand the sunlight
moving through it,

illuminating, holding the flower open like a high
clear note, an ecstatic
widening

which arrives, arrives. What
do you *do* with it? While the shrubs and the lowest
overhanging leaves

lift slightly in the wind, the blossom

doesn't move. It's the object
of affection, and this is how
it hurts you:

by holding the note open—

Past the front of the apartment, traffic goes by:
one truck, then another

comes on, disappears. And I have

the blossom *in* my vision—
  sunlight, like vision,
making clear the tiniest

hidden veins. I don't know why
I should be here, alive

and having to see this, this bright thing
living in time

or have to see it later, at the end
of the afternoon, when the sun's

lower, its light diagonal across the pot,
    its light then pulling away
across the mossed brick

like a wave, only slower,
slower. The blossom is still pink,
but no longer

brilliant. I'll go back
into the kitchen. But you, are you stronger than I? Can you
    stay in love with it? Make promises,

marry it? Are you so sure
of your position in the world?

## Brides

They must vanish of course
    who go early to the arms
of grooms. They must

take weight, who were momentarily
brilliant, crepuscular even, shining—

through a meadow, a window, a promise.

When the sun sets over the desolate beach,
the brides follow each other,

one by one, into the slow heave of the ocean. They slide
out of their gowns, escape

questions. The wind picks up;
it billows the fabric, lifts
their perfect veils.

And the surface? The surface is sweet.
It remembers them. It closes

over their delicate motions.

## There's a Man

reading late into the evening. When he looks up
a train arrives. The passengers,
who have been packed in, step off

and tuck their heads
into the cold ragged wind.
What's the story? This evening the snow was wild

and then it wasn't. A headless chicken
kept flopping about the farmhouse gate.
But maybe that was the moon
up to its moon-like tricks.

Anyhow, we're the passengers, we've come into the city
and brought with us our homemade brandy,
our peppered hams. Where is everybody?
Shouldn't there be someone here waiting?

The ones we'd thought of from the train,
from those blue fields we passed through, the empty stretches
    of Bohemia.
Where are they, the eager recipients,
the ones we'd planned on meeting at the station?

The relatives for example, waving frantically,
yelling *over here, over here!*
Where are their white handkerchiefs?
And where are they, those dear ones

who touch our hands, who bend down
and take up the packages?

## The Servant Girl

I am the fetcher of things, a strange bird
like someone named Helen or Ernestine, flicker
of purple grace, waver
and the milk leaves its skin clinging
to the edge of the pail, a little
white pond. What was it
you wanted? Barefoot girls
run shimmering over the hill,
in their summer dresses, their cotton frocks
worn from washings on rock, from afternoons
in the sun. All that it was, Greece,
is a mystery. I barely remember
the earthen jugs full of wine, the weight
of the vessel, the handle my fingers curled around,
but that there was a party once.
I carried plates of cheese.
At a banquet table beneath a grove
of sloped and gnarled olive trees, the men
slapped their palms with laughter, belched
and spoke of love. It was that which I remember,
the one who visited me, a strange boy, his back
warm from the sun beneath my palm.
I never served him. I never gave him
a single bit of wine or quartered an apple
for him to eat. But love was the boy
who lay down beneath me
and the trees and the darkening sky.

## The Wife

That's how it felt, that I was wind
leaning on everything, grieving.

And I knew how like an idiot I appeared.
I would never have you, but still
desire widened inside—
a shaking in my heart, the leaves.

Once in the middle of the night
I dreamt of your hands, that you were holding
my breasts, fingering slowly

each nipple. I curled toward you,
woke to an ache, like a knife inside
parting darknesses. A crow overhead

kept shrieking. I became that winter
a wide dark plain, the view of a house
in the distance, where all the lamps were burning,

no hope of going out.

## What Goes Through It

Of all places, tonight you're by the ocean
in a house where the windows open onto water.

The floors have been painted white
and you listen through the quiet to where

a dry snow's falling over a field
in frozen Pennsylvania, covering
   the stubble

of husks, the promise

of coal. And there's your father, hunched
and bent, saying goodnight, putting out

the light in the hall. Years go by, friendships,
desperate gestures in the same dark

going over the ocean tonight, beyond
the window. There's a breeze

through a palm, a soft

clacking, the invisible
going through it. There's a warm
rain beginning. You can stay here.

You can forgive yourself.

## Farmhouse in the Landscape

Seems like all rooms return to the kitchen,
to the four places

arranged around the table. It's winter

and where the rest are, I don't know.
It's a strangely

quiet moment, as if I'm meant to recover
something I've unknowingly lost, a woman's voice calling
    from the frayed edge

of a dream. Overhead,

the snow's crossing the roof, back and forth,
    like phrases

in a tired conversation. The woman

circles the pond in the dream. The reeds
lean together. When she opens
her mouth, it's that wide

long vowel—the sound
that will save me. A wind
cuts through oaks.

I have to focus.
I have to listen for my life

very carefully.

# Three

## The Dead

Their reward is
they become innocent again,

and when they reappear in memory
death has erased
the blurs, given them boundaries. They rise

and move through their new world with clean,
clear edges. My grandmother, in particular
has become buoyant, unattached finally

from her histories, from the trappings
of family. By no means was she

a good woman. But the dead don't care anymore for that.
Weightless, they no longer assume
responsibility, they no longer

have bodies. Once,

at the end of August, after swimming
in the muddy pond

I'd gone into the living room, cool
as vodka, where my grandmother
sat. Greed thins a woman,

and I remember her rings, bigger
than her fingers.
          Water ran down my legs

onto the floor becoming slippery
and my grandmother, her breath
scratchy from cigarettes and blended whiskey,

leaned into my ear and whispered
*you're an ugly girl.* Do I have

to forgive her? My mother tells me

no one ever loved her,
so when I see her, I see her again in the park,
in her pink tailored suit, suede pumps,

I see her moving among the strange
gentlemen that have gathered, the dark
powerful men. She is still young, blonde

and most of all, she is beyond reach, beautiful.

## Aaron Jacobson

### I

Again he returns in a dream—,
with his grandfather this time, his great-grandfather,

all of them
stalled at the same age,

in their mid-twenties, on the shore across the river,
waiting for me,

all of them tall like him, bodies
like posts, their hair straight, their hair
dark too, almost covering

their eyes. It seems they've been there for years: patient,
generations of Jacobsons

waiting for the water to row away, waiting to pick up
and come across—

### II

And why should he come back? Isn't it enough
that Aaron Jacobson exists
in Falls Church, in Virginia

with children? I didn't love him, didn't even
think it. I liked
the rifles,

the targets, the shot-up cans of Schlitz, the damage, each puncture
flared

like a little aluminum
skirt. I liked the idea of something

tearing, ripping through
the inside, the idea
of a visible wound.

Afternoons we practiced
on mattresses while overhead

gypsy moths left their white gauzy tents in the splits
    of trees. You could hear them
scratching inside; it was the beginning

of language.
    I learned to shoot that way: lying
beside him, Aaron Jacobson,

and in the Endless Mountains, there's still the smell
of burn, then the explosion up under the chest, the moan opening
    the rib cage,

and the bullet between here & there, the bullet
steady, not turning.

III

And then—
then,

I don't know what. It was years later. I could drive.
I went three hours up

to the abandoned camp. We were alone

in the lake, in water
thickened by evening. Moonlight
went sliding over the curved backs

of canoes. It shifted shadow
& boundary. I'm not lying.

I was *there*—and I can't say
what happened, if the imperative
was a command

or a plea. *Do it.* Say *naked,* or say *lake,*
*Chrysler, trees.* I don't know what to name it, the action
which is there but escapes always

through the underbrush, threads deep
into the landscape.

## Unfinished Landscape with a Dog

Not much of a dog yet,
    that smudge in the distance, beyond the reach

of focus. It's just an impressionist
gesture, a guess. From the edge of the clearing, the farmhouse
materializes, settles

into wall & stone. The water,
making the surface

of the stream, makes
reflections. So why shouldn't the dog

accept limits, become

a figure? Is it like the girl who sits
in the hall closet and says she's not
hiding? She's *inside*—

listening without the burden
of sight, letting locations

release hold. Out of body,
they seem lighter: her parents' voices no longer

hooked to their mouths. They seem
cleaner. Even the electric can opener;
the sounds of children

that rise from the yard, and fall; the opening
window, these are no longer

effects, things expected
of a subject and verb. The world anyhow is too
straightforward.

Maybe the dog
does not want to be a dog, does not want
to be turned into landscape

but to remain in the beginning, placeless:

with the wind opening, the wind
a vowel, and the stars and waters
that flash, recoil, and retch

unnamed as yet, unformed, unfound.

# Their Divorce & the Remaining Landscape

Suddenly it was silent—the snow
    scissoring through the field

and the flakes falling over stalk & husk
sounded familiar: a slight hiss, near us
but distant. We're listening,

my sister & I. We know the hedgerow
    which is thick with invisible

divisions. We know belief
is intricate. In Toledo, Ohio, a woman
takes the hotel phone off the hook

and my mother calls us in. My sister's heart
    still opens

and closes. We've been told *those people
eat garbage:* the Bissengers, Michael Schwenk,

& our fat neighbor Gloria who turns parts
into sausage, into shaped loaves
of scrapple. Behind us,

through pines, we hear the cranking
    of grinders. *I don't think*

*he loves you.* Then what in all of Pennsylvania
are we waiting for? Outside

in the wind? A return? Why, when already
we've been divided, can't stand each other

when we walk in in the continuing snow.

## Susans

Some do not have the luck
   to die young. Some become

cashiers, tellers in a bank
and take smoke breaks outside,
even in freezing wind.

They button up their rumpled coats
and vacation in the places they've dreamed of—Bermuda,
Aloha—where they've seen themselves

strolling in the distance, stepping forward
silently from the trees, smiling. Usually

Susans settle heavy into age. Their legs thicken
and spread. They become
each other, become

each other's mothers,

not like her, Susan
Derkazarian, our beautiful girl
whose neck at seventeen snapped.

Where the forces converged, she was at the heart
of the accident, in the nucleus
where all thought flocked

and snow was falling, at the silence
inside a crash—

Then the news went out
rippling through the community like a concentric
aftershock. So death, suddenly, seemed

impossible. Because what of Susan's
blonde thighs? The sound of her voice,
because what of her father's wealth

and her presence at parties
which was both familiar

and wild? Afterward,
when my boyfriend was kissing me
in basements, in a borrowed car,

when he led me into the trees
    I imagined, each time,

I was her. Then,
when he pushed my blouse aside,
my breasts

were her breasts. I wasn't shy anymore
or tired. I was a beautiful girl,

and my movements were informed
by her. So, evenings when the boy
was inside me, I held him

although I was not there. I felt finally
such sorrow for those living.

## Skating

It was Saturday,

maybe Sunday, I was smoothing my spoon across the skin
of cream of wheat

and my mother's there in the doorway, whistling
for the dogs. It was the center
of December,

the fields just hardening, our field, then Wilcox's, the corn husks
frozen in broken positions over the split earth,
and the earth uneven, unyielding, the sky

thin, the sky seemingly unable to conceive. Our father
was testing the ice,

so he walked out. The farm

sharpened. Our mother was calling,
she was whistling in the dogs. He thought the surface would work,
would hold

two girls with skates. I think I saw it then:

the wind picking up, the plastic bag
in the branches, in the future tense beginning to rip
like a ship stuck in waves. Later

the storm silenced the house, but before that

we were skating: backward, turning
awkward circles. My sister's orange tights
bagged at the knees;

I bit my glove. A strange moan
rose from under us. In the center

of December. An opening. Our mother
crazy then, screaming for the dogs. The ice

split and we fell into what freezes, consequence, already
in love with damage, with the cracks, fissures

rivering out around us, the snow falling
through the rise of pines.

# Gardening

My mother wants me to look at the agapanthus,
at the trout lily. *Look,* she says
and I look

but I hate it, the garden, all of it

from the sweep of purple violas
seeding themselves like secrets
in the shade

of the poisonous walnuts, to the heavy
stink of the lilies bent over

by the screen door. My mother
says it's labor I mind. But it isn't

labor, the hours weeding in the sun,
because I like monotony. Monotony's

a promise. It's the way she puts her face

into the flower, the way she walks through the garden
without wanting to weep.

My mother doesn't understand why I don't want
  to come home and sit

in the summer house, drinking wine,
watching the sky

abstract itself,

or watch the moonflowers that bloom later, that tremble
  in the dark.

It is always difficult to explain yourself
to the faithful.

## Late Aubade & Explanation

Once in a field, in a wide rising stretch of paintbrush
    & purple vetch, we stuck down

a tent, like punctuation, and drank through the evening
our bottle of bad wine. When you looked up,
the weather was holding: a few breezes,

a full moon silvering the flowers

to white. In the distance, I heard the ache
& slide of snow, the beginning of crickets. It was twilight—

the landscape was lifting.


.


                A mountain. The clouds, further up,
came down. A Book of Hours. A tent in which we twisted,
pressed each against the other, drunk

and when I stepped out into the cool
moonlight, there was drifting through the watery
end of the meadow, a deer

pale beneath pines, beneath those soaring
darknesses. Then there was only darkness, the
idea of a deer.

        Remember, I never wanted
to be alive, to have
an outline. Better, I knew, to slip

unheld, an opening into mist.

## Hiding

*—to my sister*

Because the moon in late October made landmarks glow: the broken
    gate, our yard

full of stones, the attic window

suddenly foreign, across its face
a blue dissolve. In spite of that, the farm

remained an arrangement (barn
behind the house, pond
across the road) and a girl sometimes

feels torn. We turned our dresses inside out,
ran into a grove. We played

*you're blind, Molly, try to find me.*
It was a family game: get left

in darkness. I climbed
up into the oak, listened for your voice
until my name became

a sound from the other side, from the poor
order of the world. I came back

because I had to. And believe me, you who are fragile
and so faithful, I hated to return

materializing through trees.

KATE NORTHROP is an assistant professor of English/Creative Writing at West Chester University in Pennsylvania. Her poems have been published in *Painted Bride, Raritan, Michigan Quarterly Review, Northwest Review, The Dark Horse, Quarterly West, Rattle, Louisiana Literature,* and *Black Warrior Review.* She has received many honors including the Pennsylvania Council of the Arts Individual Artist Fellowship, the Greater Philadelphia Cultural Alliance Grant, and the 1995 American Academy of Poets Prize, University of Iowa.